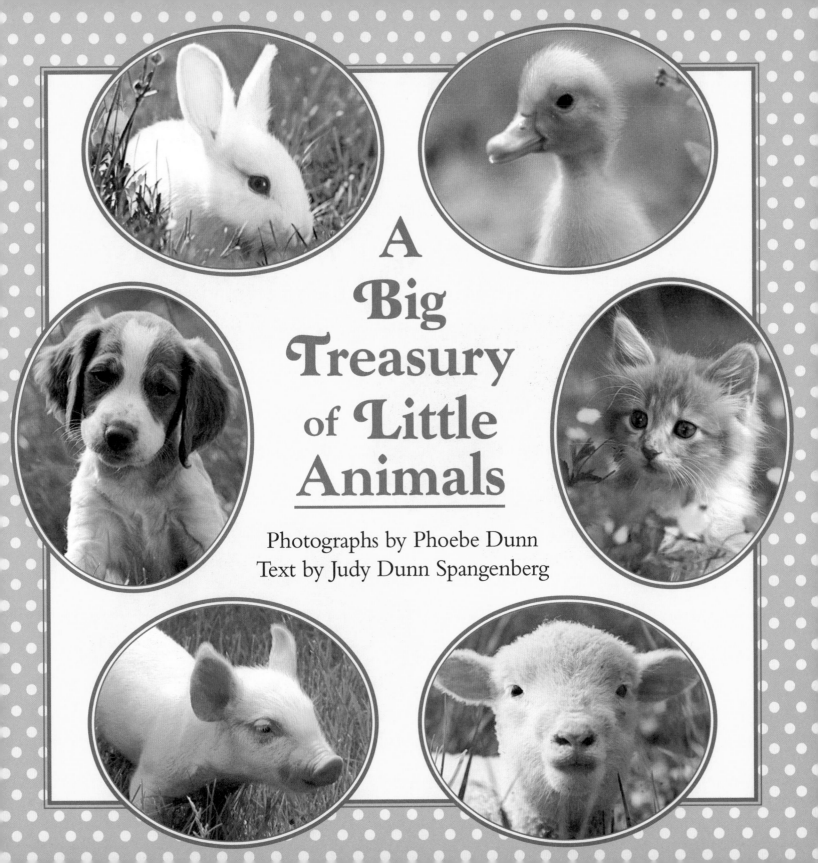

A Big Treasury of Little Animals

Photographs by Phoebe Dunn
Text by Judy Dunn Spangenberg

The Little Rabbit

The Little Duck

The Little Pig

Phoebe Dunn

was a world-renowned photographer known especially for her pictures of children and animals. Her timeless images, photographed in natural settings, using natural light, uniquely capture the interactions and relationships between children and their pets.

Phoebe Dunn's photographs have been published around the world in more than twenty children's books, a number of them written by her daughter, Judy Dunn. For more than thirty years, Phoebe Dunn photographed the world as she knew it, capturing the feelings and relationships that make us all human.

The Little Lamb

One afternoon in early spring,
Emmy walked over to the
Wetherbee Farm.

There were twenty newborn
lambs in the flock, and Emmy
couldn't wait to see them.

All the lambs had long, wobbly legs and little pointed hooves.
Most of them were white, but a few were black. Emmy stood
on a rock and watched them follow their mothers into the barn.

Mother sheep usually keep their babies close to them. But one little white lamb wandered away from the flock. He seemed to be lost. *Baa-baa-baa*, he cried.

Emmy jumped off the rock and the little lamb ran right up to her.

Mrs. Wetherbee asked Emmy if she would like to take care of the lamb until he was big enough to come back to the flock. He had a twin brother, and their mother did not have enough milk for two babies.

Emmy was so happy she bent over and kissed the little lamb. Then she gently picked him up and carried him home.

He was cuddly and warm, and she could feel his heart beating. Emmy decided to call her lamb Timothy.

That evening Emmy heated milk for her lamb. She sat down under the maple tree and gave him his bottle.

At first he wiggled and chewed the rubber nipple. Warm milk dripped all over Emmy. But Timothy quickly learned to sit still and drink his milk.

Emmy was a good mother to Timothy. She fed him twice a day and gave him plenty of love. Soon Timothy followed Emmy wherever she went.

By summertime the little lamb didn't need to drink milk from a bottle anymore. He was big enough to eat grain out of a dish. His fleece had grown thick and woolly.

Emmy put a collar and bell around Timothy's neck. He slept in the barn, curled up in the warm straw outside the horse's stall.

On sunny summer days, Emmy and Timothy went to the fields together. While they played hide-and-seek, Midnight the cat chased after bumblebees.

Emmy would hide in the tall grass. But sooner or later, Timothy always found her.

When Timothy was tired, he
plopped down to rest on Emmy's lap.

Sometimes Emmy liked to make dandelion chains and pretend she was a princess. The only trouble was— Timothy ate the dandelions.

When Emmy wasn't around to play, Timothy always seemed to get into mischief.

He would rub his back against the sheets on the clothesline, or jump into the laundry basket for a nap.

One morning Timothy tipped over a basket on the porch. *Bumpity-bumpity-bump.* A whole bushel of apples bounced down the steps.

Then Timothy scampered into the garden. He ate the tops off all the radishes and trampled the lettuce plants.

After that he started eating the primroses.

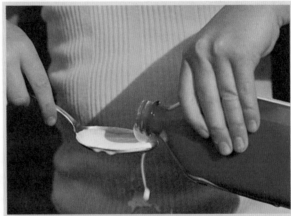

Emmy found Timothy hiding behind the house—full of vegetables and flowers and feeling quite sick. She poured some medicine into a spoon and Timothy swallowed it all.

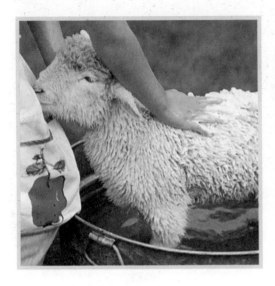

The next day Timothy was feeling fine. Emmy decided to give him a bath. She wanted him to look his best because they were going to a birthday party.

Emmy filled the washtub with warm, soapy water and scrubbed Timothy's ears and chin. She shampooed his fleece until it was soft and white.

Then she rubbed him down with a fuzzy towel. Later on, when he was dry, she combed his woolly coat.

Emmy's father drove them to the party in his truck. Emmy was wearing her party dress, and Timothy had a new purple leash.

The birthday party was lots of fun. All the children wore paper hats, and bright balloons hung over the table.

When the children sat down for ice cream and cake, Emmy tied her lamb to the table to keep him close.

Suddenly . . . BANG . . . a balloon popped!

The loud noise
frightened Timothy.
He tried to run away.

The table collapsed,
the ice cream spilled,
and the cake slid to the
ground.

What a mess!

That evening Emmy's
father said Timothy was
getting too big to keep
as a pet.

Early the next morning,
Emmy walked Timothy to
the Wetherbee Farm.
　　She hugged Timothy's
woolly neck and promised
to visit whenever she could.

Then she took off his purple leash and Timothy scampered out to meet the flock.

He buried his nose in a clover patch, and grazed with the other sheep in the morning sun.

Timothy was back where he belonged.
Now there were twenty lambs again at
the Wetherbee Farm.

The Little Puppy

im felt lonely. Summer vacation was
starting and there was no one nearby for
him to play with.

Then one day, early in the summer, Tim
heard some exciting news. The next-door
neighbor's dog had just had six puppies.
Tim had always wanted a dog.

Every day Tim went next door to see the puppies. He begged his parents to let him have one. Finally they agreed.

Tim could hardly wait to bring his puppy home. But the puppies were still too small to leave their mother.

Tim and his father built
a bed for the puppy. They
measured and sawed and
hammered until it was perfect.

"A puppy is a lot of work, Tim," said his father. "You will have to take care of it every day."

Tim promised that he would. Then he painted the puppy's box all by himself.

At last the puppies were old enough to leave their mother. Tim went next door to pick one out. He played with each puppy and tried to choose his favorite. But it was hard. All the puppies were wiggly and warm and friendly.

"Maybe I'll take *you* home," Tim said to one puppy.

"Or maybe you," he said to another. He just couldn't decide which one he wanted.

But Tim never did get to choose a puppy—because one little puppy chose him! The puppy stretched up to lick Tim's chin. Tim picked him up gently. The puppy wagged his stubby tail.

"Now, what will I name you?" wondered Tim. He thought hard. Finally he said, "You look like Charlie to me."

Tim carried Charlie to his new home.

Charlie was lonely the first night in his new bed. He missed his brothers and sisters. Tim put a ticking alarm clock in the bed to keep Charlie company, but the puppy still whined and howled.

Charlie saw Tim's toy dog lying on the floor. It was just what the lonely puppy needed. He jumped out of bed and dragged the toy into his box. Then he flopped down on its soft back and was soon fast asleep.

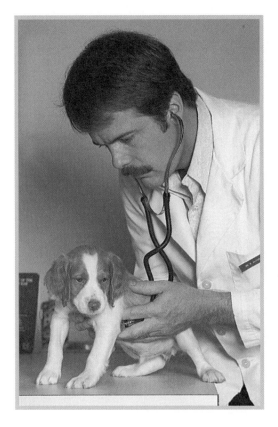

The next day Tim took Charlie to see the vet. Dr. McFarland listened to the puppy's heart and gave him a shot to keep him healthy.

Charlie didn't bark or cry once. "Good dog," said Tim, and he patted his brave puppy.

Charlie soon got used to his new home. He liked to explore all the new things.

Tim and Charlie were usually together all day. But once Tim left Charlie alone on the porch. That was a mistake.

Charlie sniffed some flowers in a pot and—*whoops!*—what a mess!
Then the little puppy jumped up on a chair with his dirty feet. When Tim found him, he gave Charlie a big scolding.

Tim and Charlie had lots of fun together. Charlie's favorite toy was a squishy red ball. Tim would roll it across the lawn, and Charlie would chase it as fast as he could.

Charlie would grab the ball with his teeth and carry it back to Tim. Then the game would begin again.

Sometimes, though, Charlie forgot to let go of the ball!

Near the end of the summer Tim visited his grandfather at
the lake. Of course, Charlie went with him. They both liked to
sit on the dock in the warm sun.

Charlie wasn't allowed to go in the rowboat with Grandpa and Tim.

"You don't know how to swim," Tim said. "You can come with us next summer."

But Charlie couldn't wait that long.

SPLASH! He paddled after the boat.

Grandpa pulled Charlie out of the water. The little puppy was wet and shivering. Grandpa dried him off and wrapped him in a soft towel to keep him warm. The puppy was all tired out.

The next day Charlie went along in the rowboat. "He sure fooled us!" Tim said. "He doesn't need any swimming lessons."

Autumn came and Tim went back to school. Charlie didn't understand why his friend left him every day. The first day he howled.

But Charlie learned to wait patiently on the porch for Tim. As soon as he saw Tim walking up the street, he raced to meet him.

Every afternoon Tim romped with Charlie before doing his homework. The pup was big enough to play football now. He loved to grab the ball from Tim and run away with it.

Touchdown for Charlie!

When Tim had to rake leaves, Charlie thought it was a new game.

"Hey, cut it out, Charlie!" Tim laughed.

Now Charlie was big enough to go on long walks with Tim. One sunny weekend they went exploring in the woods.

The woods were full of the scents of animals. Charlie wanted to follow them. Tim took off his leash.

Charlie sniffed along the ground and into holes.

One scent led him to a raccoon!

Charlie barked wildly and chased it up a tree.

Tim and Charlie did everything together. "You're my
best friend, Charlie," said Tim. "We'll be friends forever."
Charlie looked at Tim and wagged his tail.

The Little Kitten

Jenny's cat was restless. It was time for her kittens to be born. She looked in the barn for a comfortable spot to have her kittens, but the straw was much too scratchy. She prowled all over the house and yard. But nothing seemed to suit her.

So Jenny made a soft bed for her cat in the bottom drawer of her bureau. That night six fluffy kittens were born there.

Jenny's cat was a good mother. She nursed her kittens when they were hungry and washed them with her rough pink tongue.

At first the kittens seemed to sleep all day. But in a few weeks they were tumbling all over one another. When the mother cat wanted a little peace, she crouched under the drawer.

One little kitten was more curious than the others. He was the first to try his wobbly legs.

He was the first to peek over the edge of the drawer.

And he was the first to climb out of the bureau. PLOP! He fell to the floor. But Jenny found him and scooped him up before he had a chance to get into trouble.

Jenny's mother promised that she could keep one of the kittens. They would find new homes for the others.

Jenny loved every one of the kittens, but she loved the curious kitten most of all.

"You're my favorite!" she said to the kitten.

Meow, the kitten answered softly.

Jenny made a bed for her kitten in a special basket. The kitten tried it out right away. He was still little and needed lots of naps. When he woke up, he was ready to go exploring.

The curious kitten scampered through the house. He found Father's sneakers and tried to squeeze inside. But already he was too big to fit. The kitten was growing very fast.

Soon the kitten was old enough to drink milk from a dish. At first he didn't know what to do. He stepped right into it! Milk stuck to his paws and dripped from his chin.

"Oh, what a pickle you're in!" said Jenny when she saw the milky kitten.

Saying that gave her an idea. "I'm going to call you Pickle," she told her kitten. It turned out to be a very good name for him.

The curious kitten got into one pickle after another. One day he wanted to see what was inside a can of flour.

What a mess that made! Pickle looked so funny that Jenny didn't even mind cleaning up after him.

Jenny played with her kitten every day. One night she gave him a catnip mouse. It made the kitten do silly things.

First he sniffed the mouse. . . .

Then he batted it . . .
and clawed it . . . and licked
it . . . and chewed it . . . and
rolled it around on the floor!

Soon the mouse was in
shreds and the kitten was all
tired out.

Jenny let Pickle sleep on
her bed just this once. The
little kitten curled up beside
her and purred. He was happy
to be with Jenny.

One sunny day Jenny took her kitten outdoors. She wanted
him to keep her company while she planted some flowers. Pickle
tried to see everything she was doing. He kept getting in the way.

Finally Jenny picked
up the kitten and put
him in a flowerpot.
"Now stay there,"
she scolded.

But Pickle was too curious
to stay anywhere for long.
He jumped out of the
flowerpot and set off on an
adventure.

Pickle wandered into the meadow, where he felt safe in
the tall grass. He hardly knew where to look first. There were
so many sights and sounds and smells that were new to him.

He discovered a turtle sunning itself on a rock . . . a praying mantis waiting to catch an insect for lunch . . . and two baby squirrels climbing a tree and chattering to each other.

A baby rabbit was hiding under a mushroom. The rabbit sat very still and hoped the kitten wouldn't notice him.

Wild strawberries grew in the meadow. So did lots of flowers. The kitten watched a caterpillar inch up the stem of a Queen Anne's lace.

Beyond the meadow Pickle climbed onto a woodpile. He found lots of hiding places in it.

Then he tried to squeeze into an empty woodchuck hole but got stuck halfway!

Meow, meow! he cried.

Jenny finally heard him and came to his rescue.

"Please don't get into any more trouble," she begged.

After that she held her kitten very close whenever she took him outdoors.

Pickle liked Jenny's attention. But he liked to explore
even better. It wasn't long before he slipped away again.
This time he practiced walking on the orchard fence.
He had a good sense of balance, so he didn't fall once.

Then Pickle scrambled up
an apple tree. Climbing up was
easy, but he was too frightened
to climb back down.

Meow, he called.
Mee-oww-w.

"Oh, Pickle, you're in a pickle again!" said Jenny when she found him.

She dragged a box out to the tree and gently helped the little kitten down.

"Now don't go off again!" said Jenny.

Pickle snuggled up to her and purred. He seemed to be saying that he'd had enough exploring.

But the very next day he was off again! Jenny took him to a birthday party, and when the children weren't watching, Pickle wandered away. They finally found him snoozing in the doghouse.

"What *am* I going to do with you?" Jenny asked her kitten.
Suddenly she had an idea. . . .

"Now you can't hide from me, Pickle!"

The Little Rabbit

One Easter, Sarah found a little rabbit in her Easter basket. She was nestled beside two eggs.

The little rabbit was soft and white. She had bright pink eyes, long ears that were pink inside, and a tiny pink nose that was always wiggling. Sarah loved her new friend very much.

Sarah let the little rabbit play in the grass while she tried to think of just the right name for her. There were some tiny yellow flowers nearby called buttercups. "That's a nice name!" said Sarah to her little friend. "I'll call *you* Buttercup, too."

Sarah took good care of Buttercup. Every day she visited the new red hutch, bringing food pellets and fresh water. Then she watched Buttercup eat and drink.

Sarah's other friends loved Buttercup, too. After school they hurried over to Sarah's house and played with the little rabbit. Buttercup was always happy to be the center of attention. All the children wished they had a rabbit of their own.

One afternoon Sarah took
Buttercup out to the meadow and
fell asleep. But Buttercup did not
want to sleep. She was soon
hopping off to meet new friends.
First she came upon a slow-moving
turtle, and then she met a
beautiful orange and black
butterfly. There was so much to
see and do out in the world.

But what was *that*! Buttercup was startled by something moving in the ferns. It was another rabbit.

The other rabbit was a wild rabbit. He was quite different from Buttercup. He had large brown eyes and brown fur that helped him to hide from his enemies. The two rabbits watched each other for a long time. Then they hopped away.

Buttercup was hungry,
so she nibbled some grass
beside a rhubarb patch.
Suddenly it began to rain.
She ran for cover and got
stuck between some stalks.
Then she sat and watched
the rain. She felt very
small and very lonely.

When Sarah woke up, she searched all over for Buttercup and finally found her.

Sarah and Buttercup went everywhere together. Sometimes they went on picnics in the woods. Sarah always brought along a carrot for Buttercup.

Sarah was very proud of her rabbit. Over the next few months Buttercup grew bigger and bigger. Soon she was ready to have babies of her own. Sarah put a nesting box filled with clean straw into the hutch.

Buttercup pulled fur from her coat to make a soft, warm nest for her babies. Then she waited. Sarah visited the hutch often, but nothing happened.

Then one morning
Sarah looked into the
hutch and saw seven
baby rabbits in the nest.
  "Oh, Buttercup," she
said, "you're a mother!"
Sarah was so happy to
see the babies.

The babies grew fast. Soon they were big enough to climb out of the nesting box and look around. They were lively and curious, and as soft and white as their mother. Now Sarah had to think of names for all of them!

Since there were seven baby rabbits, Sarah decided to name them after the seven days of the week— Sunday, Monday, Tuesday, Wednesday, Thursday, Friday, and Saturday.

Soon the little rabbits were big enough to go outside. Sunday, Monday, and Tuesday stayed in Sarah's lap, but the others jumped out. Wednesday sat under the daffodils, Thursday sniffed violets, and Friday hopped through the grass.

Little Saturday went farther than any of her brothers and sisters. Soon she found herself in a sea of tiny blue flowers. There were flowers everywhere. Saturday stopped right where she was because she didn't know what else to do. She was lost, but Sarah soon found her.

It was time for the rabbits to go home. Sarah couldn't get them all back by herself, so she called for her father. Together they collected the little rabbits and put them back into the hutch with Buttercup.

"Sarah," said her father, "there are just too many rabbits, and they're getting bigger every day. It's time you found good homes for Buttercup's babies." Sarah wanted to keep them all, but she knew her father was right. There *were* too many rabbits, and the hutch was crowded.

So the next day Sarah offered one or two of Buttercup's babies to each of her friends. Monday went home with Kate, and Billy chose Tuesday for his pet.

Wednesday and Thursday rode home in Jeff's bicycle basket. By the end of the day, all of Buttercup's babies had new homes, and Sarah's friends were proud to have rabbits of their own.

Sarah and Buttercup were happy to be alone
together, just as they were in the beginning.
"I love you, Buttercup," said Sarah as she
stroked her rabbit's soft white fur. But Buttercup
just wiggled her pink nose.

The Little Duck

One morning in early spring, a little boy was fishing in the pond near his farm. Again and again he threw out his line and pulled it in. At last he caught a fish.

The boy gathered his things to go home. Suddenly he saw something nestled in the tall grass at the pond's edge. It was an egg—a duck's egg. The little boy carried the egg home with him.

He placed the egg in an incubator so it would keep warm. Every day the boy turned the egg over as gently as a mother duck.

Finally, after twenty-eight days of waiting and watching, the boy heard something peeping and pecking inside the egg. The shell cracked . . . and broke open. Henry, the little duck, was hatched.

Henry did not
look at all as the boy
thought he should.

His feathers were wet, and
they stuck to his body. His feet
were enormous.

The little duck stood
up on his big orange feet.
He tried a few small steps.

Then he stretched his
spindly wings and wiggled
them as fast as he could. He
began to get dry and fluffy.

Getting hatched is hard work. Henry was tired. He put his head down beside his empty shell and went to sleep. When Henry woke up, his fluffy yellow down was completely dry. Now he looked like a duck.

After a few days the boy placed him in a wading pool. It was time for the little duck's first swim. Henry tried hard to paddle. But the more he paddled, the deeper he sank.

Ducks cannot float without oil on their feathers. Baby ducks usually get this oil from their mother's feathers when she sits in the nest with them.

But Henry's mother was an incubator. He would have to wait until his own oil glands began to work before he tried to swim again.

The boy quickly scooped Henry up from the bottom of the pool and wrapped him in a towel. Henry was shivering and sputtering.

The boy was afraid he would catch cold.
So he set the hairdryer on "warm" and
dried Henry's feathers in no time.

When the little duck was dry
again, he found a cozy resting place
on the broad back of the family dog.
Together they dozed in the sunshine.

Through the summer Henry kept growing. The boy fed him cracked corn and duck mash. The more Henry ate, the bigger he grew.

One day as Henry was standing beside a puddle, his reflection showed stiff white feathers growing over his yellow down.

Suddenly Henry's voice began to do something new. While he was small, *peep peep* was all he said. But now strange noises came out when he opened his beak: *Peep peep squank. Peep quonk. Peep quack quack quack.*

Henry was growing up.

During the summer Henry followed the boy all around the farm.

Sometimes the boy was busy. Then Henry looked for other friends. One day he waddled down the hill and into the barnyard. He quacked at the hen. But the hen did not care about ducks.

He quacked at the rabbit. The rabbit listened, but did not say anything. When Henry quacked at the goat, the goat leaned over and butted him. Finally Henry went back home.

Summer turned into autumn and the boy had to go to school. Without anyone to play with, Henry had nothing to do all day. He tried to swim in his blue plastic pool. But the pool had become too small for Henry.

On weekends the boy stayed
home. Then Henry was happy.
He had a playmate.

And sometimes, on warm
winter days when the boy was
away, his grandfather would rock
Henry on the porch.

But still Henry seemed lonely.
He needed a special friend. The
little duck was almost grown up.

One bright morning in early spring, Henry waddled off the porch.

He was a handsome grown-up duck now, with a beautiful curled feather at the tip of his tail.

Henry walked straight down the hill, past the barnyard, and across the meadow.

Suddenly Henry stopped. He opened his beak in a loud quack. Before him was a wide, deep pool of water—much wider and deeper than his blue plastic pool at home. Henry had found the pond.

In the middle of the pond, spreading its wings, was the first duck Henry had ever seen.

As fast as he could, Henry paddled out to meet
the new duck. It looked almost exactly like Henry.
But it did not have a special curl at the tip of its tail.

The duck was a girl. She quacked at Henry.
Henry had found his special friend at last.

Soon Henry and his friend had
an egg of their own, nestled in the
tall grass beside the pond.

The Little Pig

Early one spring a litter of baby pigs was born at Apple Tree Farm, down the road from Michael's house.

Every day after school Michael rode his bike to the farm and watched the piglets play. They always looked like they were having so much fun.

One little pig was much smaller than the rest. The mother pig paid special attention to her and even gave her extra milk when the other piglets weren't watching.

This little pig was Michael's favorite. He liked to call her Lucy. More than anything, he wanted to bring Lucy home with him and take care of her. But the farmer said she wasn't big enough—at least not yet.

But little by little, Lucy got pinker and plumper. And at last the day came when she was ready to go home with Michael. Michael put her in a big basket filled with straw so Lucy would be comfortable on the bumpy ride home.

Michael thought Lucy would stay put, but Lucy had other ideas. *Whoops!* Before he knew it, Lucy had tipped over the basket and away she ran.

Michael scooped her up just in time. After that he held on to the basket and Lucy until they reached his house.

Right away Michael took Lucy to her new pen. He carried in two big armloads of straw, then put Lucy inside.

Oink! Oink! Oink! Lucy squealed over and over again. She seemed to like her new home.

Freckles came to see what all the noise was about. He had never seen a pig before. But soon they were rubbing noses like old friends.

Then Lucy burrowed under the straw. Maybe she was trying to play hide-and-seek. What a funny little pig!

Michael soon found out that Lucy was a pig who liked to do things her way. The next day he took her out into the field. Michael could tell that Lucy was hungry, so he brought along a bottle of warm milk. But would she drink from the bottle? No!

Then Michael had an idea. He poured some milk into a dish. Lucy slurped up every drop.

"Good piggy!" said Michael. "Now you'll grow."

Michael loved Lucy even though she was difficult at times. He built Lucy a sturdy wooden house of her very own. As soon as the paint was dry, the little pig moved in and made herself right at home.

Lucy liked her new house. But she liked Freckles's house even better. Sometimes Lucy would jump in and out of the doghouse over and over again. She thought it was a game.

Freckles was very patient with Lucy even when she decided to take a nap inside his house. He always sat and waited until she came out again.

Lucy was a very curious little pig. She loved to get her snout into everything—especially dirt!

Lucy also loved to go exploring. Lots of times she wandered off into the fields. There were always flowers to smell and insects to watch.

One day Lucy wandered off too far. She grew very hot and very tired.

It was too far to walk back home, so Lucy lay down in the cool grass and waited for Michael to come and get her.

Oink! Oink! she called out to him.

At last Michael found her. Lucy just smiled up at him, flopped down in his lap, and went right to sleep.

One day two of Michael's friends came over for a picnic.
Lucy was taking a nap inside her house. Michael was glad.
"We don't need Lucy around to mess up our picnic," he
said, and his friends agreed.

But Lucy was not asleep for long. The children were so busy talking and eating that they did not notice the little pig sneaking out of her house.

Lucy headed straight for the picnic basket. Very quietly she poked her snout inside. The first thing she found was a bag of chocolate cookies—her favorites! One, two, three, Lucy gobbled them up!

Oink! Oink! Lucy squealed happily.

"Lucy!" cried Michael. "I should have known you wouldn't miss a picnic."

There was nothing else Lucy wanted in the basket, so she knocked it over and waddled across the blanket. She ate a peanut butter sandwich and some watermelon.

Michael looked at his friends and laughed. "Lucy sure made a pig of herself at our picnic!"

One afternoon Michael saw a sign for a pet show. The pet show was going to be held the very next day. He was sure Lucy would never win a prize. She was much too naughty and squealy. But he thought it might be fun to go anyway. Lucy would need a bath right away, so Michael went to find her.

Was Lucy in her house? No, of course not. She was never where she was supposed to be.

Was she in Freckles's house? No, she was not there, either.

Michael finally found Lucy eating his mother's flowers. Michael grabbed the little pig.

"Gotcha!" he said. "You are getting a bath now."

Lucy struggled to get away. Michael had to hold her tight. His little pig had grown much bigger and stronger.

Michael carried a bucket
of warm water for Lucy's
bath. He was very careful not
to get soap in her eyes while
he scrubbed her.

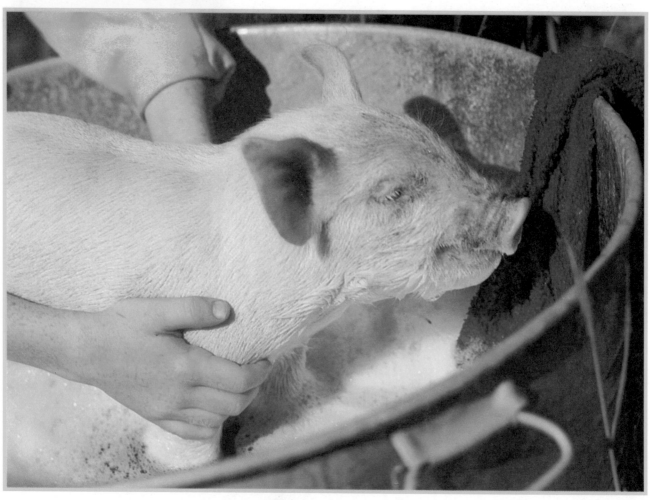

But still Lucy kept squealing and trying to get away. At last the little pig was clean. Michael carried her back to her pen.

"Now you stay put!" Michael told Lucy.

The next day was the
pet show. Michael got out
his old red wagon and put
Lucy in it.

But Lucy did not want to ride in
the wagon, so Michael tried Freckles's
leash. And that worked just fine.

It was a very hot day, and on the
way to the pet show Michael let Lucy
take a swim. She *really* liked that!

When they got to the pet show, the other contestants were already there. One boy had brought his box turtle. Another was carrying a soft brown bunny. Michael's neighbor was there with her puppy.

The children had to show their pets to the judge. Michael waited and waited. It was hot, and Lucy started to squeal. "Please behave," Michael whispered to her.

At last it was Lucy's turn. The judge leaned over to look at Lucy.

Oink! Oink! she squealed, and then she hid under the table.

"Lucy, please come out," said Michael. But Lucy wouldn't budge. Michael should have known Lucy would do something like this.

Now it was time for the judge to announce the winners. Everyone waited patiently. Michael was sure Lucy would not win a prize—not the way she had behaved.

A fluffy orange kitten won third prize. A goldfish won second.

"And now for first prize," said the judge. "It goes to Lucy the pig."

Michael couldn't believe it when the judge pinned the blue ribbon right on Lucy's harness.

"That's a smart little pig you have," the judge told Michael.
"She knew it was too hot in the sun, so she stayed in the shade
under my table."

Michael walked Lucy home. He felt so proud. The sky
was as blue as Lucy's blue ribbon. What a wonderful day!